Presented to

T. J. Drake

Date

August 21, 2001

From

Brite Teachers

My See, Point, and Learn

BIBLE BOOK

MY SEE, POINT, AND LEARN BIBLE Book

My See, Point, and Learn

BIBLE BOOK

An Interactive Picture-Reading Adventure

by Mary Hollingsworth

Illustrated by
Marlene McAuley

BAKER BOOK HOUSE
Grand Rapids, Michigan

Contents

Page

Dear Parents and Teachers,

Have you ever wished young children could read before they can actually read? Well, now they can! In truth, young children read things every day, even before they can identify printed words on a page. They read situations; they read people; they read pictures; they read life.

My See, Point, and Learn Bible Book gives pre-readers the chance to do what they already know how to do—read pictures, people, situations, and life. Through a series of questions provided for the adult reader to ask, young children will be able to explore biblical and contemporary stories on their own to grasp the virtues and values being taught.

This great new interactive book draws young children into the colorful pictures and lets them tell what's happening in the stories. At the same time, the questions and statements reinforce the values they are learning. The child will be applauded for right thinking and cheered into godly behavior. Then the "Remember Rhyme" at the end of each two-page section will serve as a memory device to help children retain the valuable teaching and put it into everyday use.

In addition to spiritual values and morals, this delightful new book will help your young child learn to count, identify colors, name animals, make animal sounds, sing songs, and pray. All in all, *My See, Point, and Learn Bible Book* is lots of fun, as well as being an excellent teacher. Your child will love it, and so will you.

Teachers, you will find this new resource especially valuable in the classroom, too. Young children will love to "Hooray!" for right and "Boo!" for wrong, as well as answer the questions about the stories. A great supplement for Sunday school curriculum, this new pre-reader's Bible book gives you a ready-made supply of fresh approaches to familiar Bible stories and teachings.

If you think *My See, Point, and Learn Bible Book* is an outstanding addition to a young child's bookshelf, say, "Hooray for me!" We pray it will bless the lives of young children everywhere.

The Publisher

Be a Friend

Let's Read the Picture

1. There are some soldiers in this picture. Can you count the soldiers?

2. The soldiers are taking Jesus away. Point to Jesus.

3. Can you find Jesus' friend Peter in the picture?

4. What is the woman with Peter doing?

5. Is Peter being a friend to Jesus?

6. Should you always be a friend to Jesus?

7. Will Jesus always be a friend to you? Say, "Hooray for Jesus!"

"A friend loves at all times." Proverbs 17:17

. These two boys are Michael and Joey. What are the boys in the picture doing?

. Do you think these two boys are friends? Why? Say, "Hooray for friends!"

. How many boys are in the picture?

4. What colors are the leaves?

5. Can you point to some other friends in the picture?

6. Should real friends be friends *all* the time or just *some* of the time?

Remember Rhyme

Don't pretend, be a friend!

15

Be Brave

Let's Read the Picture

1. Point to the bear in the picture. Say, "Grrrrr!" Don't let it get you! (Hug the child tight.)

2. What color is the bear?

3. There are some sheep in the picture, too. Say, "Baa." Can you count them?

4. Point to the shepherd. His name is David.

5. What is the shepherd doing?

6. Do you think the shepherd is being brave? Say, "Hooray for David!"

7. How do you know that David is brave?

8. Can you tell about a time when *you* were brave? (When the child finishes telling, say, "Hooray for you!")

16

1. Point to the little girl in the picture. Her name is Maria. Say, "Hi, Maria."

2. Who else is in this picture? Her name is Doctor Jill. Say, "Hi, Doctor Jill."

3. What is the doctor doing? Say, "Aw, that didn't hurt."

4. Is Maria being brave? Say, "Hooray for Maria!"

5. How can you tell that she is being brave?

6. Who else in the picture has a hurt place? But is Teddy smiling and being brave anyway? Say, "Hooray for Teddy!"

7. Are you brave when you have to go to the doctor or wear a bandage? (If the child says yes, say, "Hooray for you!")

Remember Rhyme

Don't rant and rave; be strong and brave!

17

Be Fair

Let's Read the Picture

1. Lazarus is the poor man in this picture. Can you point to Lazarus? Say, "Awwww."

2. Where is the *rich* man?

3. What is the rich man doing?

4. Does he have lots of nice food? Say, "Mmm mmm good."

5. Does Lazarus have any food? Say, "Awwww."

6. Is the rich man sharing his food with Lazarus?

7. Is the rich man being fair? Say, "Booo on unfairness!"

8. How could the rich man be fair with Lazarus?

18

1. Point to the little girl in the picture. Her name is Chen. Say, "Hi, Chen."

2. The boy is her big brother Lee. What is Lee doing?

3. Is he being fair with his sister? Say, "Booo for being unfair!"

4. How do you know he is not being fair?

5. Can you count the squirrels in the picture?

6. What color are the squirrels?

7. Is the squirrel with the nut being fair to the other squirrel? Say, "Hooray for the squirrel!"

8. How do you know?

Remember Rhyme *Always dare to be completely fair!*

Be Gentle

Let's Read the Picture

1. Jacob is sitting in Jesus' lap. Do you think Jesus is being kind and gentle to Jacob? Say, "Hooray for Jesus!"

2. Jesus is telling a story. Point to some one who is listening.

3. Who else in the picture seems to be listening to Jesus? Can you say, "Oink, oink"?

4. Does Jesus love all children and animals? Say, "Thank you, Jesus."

5. Does he want *you* to be gentle with animals, too?

6. What do you think it means to be gentle?

7. Are you gentle with your friends and family? (If the child says yes, say, "Hooray for you!")

"Let all men see that you are gentle and kind." Philippians 4:5

1. This little girl is Jenna. What is Jenna doing?

2. Bunnies are cuddly and soft. (Cuddle the child and give a little tickle.)

3. Is Jenna being gentle with the bunny? Say, "Hooray for Jenna!"

4. How do you know she's being gentle?

5. How many other bunnies are in the picture? Can you count them?

6. Bunnies like to eat clover. Can you point to the clover?

7. What color is the clover?

8. Are you always kind and gentle to little animals? (If the child says yes, say, "Hooray for you!")

Remember Rhyme

Gentle ways are happy ways.

21

Be Happy

Let's Read the Picture

1. The bride in this picture is named Ruth. The groom is named Boaz. Do they look happy? Say, "Ahhh."

2. What are Ruth and Boaz doing? Say, "Hooray for Ruth and Boaz!"

3. Point to someone else who looks happy. Her name is Naomi. Say, "Hi, Naomi."

4. Who is the other man in the picture?

5. Do you think Ruth and Boaz love each other? Say, "Ahhh."

6. Is love what makes them happy?

7. Who loves *you?* (When the child answers, hug the child and say, *"I love you!"*)

"Happy are the people whose God is the Lord." Psalm 144:15

1. Can you count the children in this picture?

2. Are the children happy? Say, "Hooray for the children!"

3. How do you know they are happy?

4. Where are the children?

5. What are the children doing? (Sing a verse of "If You're Happy and You Know It" together.)

6. Do you think they are singing because they are happy?

7. What do *you* do when you are happy? (After the child tells, say, "Hooray for you!")

Remember Rhyme *Being good's the only way to live happy every day!*

Be Honest

Let's Read the Picture

1. The little boy in this picture is named Benjamin. Can you point to him?

2. Why is Benjamin running away?

3. Who is angry in the picture?

4. Is Benjamin being honest? Say, "Booo for dishonesty!"

5. Is God happy when we steal something?

6. Can you tell about a time when something was stolen?

7. Should you ever steal things? Let's pray and ask God to help us never to steal. (Pray with the child.)

"...you can easily see if I am honest."
Genesis 30:33

1. How many girls are in this picture? Their names are Sally and Connie. Say, "Hi, Connie. Hi, Sally."

2. Connie and Sally have found something. What have they found?

3. What is in the wallet?

4. Can you point to the policeman?

5. Are the girls being honest? Say, "Hooray for Sally and Connie!"

6. How do you know they are being honest?

7. Why is the policeman smiling?

8. Is God happy when you are honest, too? Say, "Hooray for me!"

Remember Rhyme

An honest me is a happy me.

25

Be Kind

Let's Read the Picture

1. How many ladies are in the picture? Can you count them?

2. Dorcas likes to sew. Can you point to the new coat she has made? Say, "Ohhhh, that's pretty."

3. What color is the new coat?

4. Who else in the picture has Dorcas been kind to? Say, "Hooray for Dorcas!"

5. Are the ladies happy with the presents Dorcas has given them?

6. How do you know they are happy?

7. Is it good to be kind and loving to others?

8. Do you know someone who is kind? (When the child answers, say, "Hooray for_____!")

"Be kind and loving to each other." Ephesians 4:32

1. Can you count the ducks in the picture?

2. What color are the ducks?

3. The man's name is Grandpa Jerry. Is the man being kind to the ducks? Say, "Hooray for Grandpa Jerry!"

4. What is he doing to be kind?

5. Who else is being kind? Her name is Marcy. Say, "Hooray for Marcy!"

6. How is she showing kindness?

7. Can you tell about a time when you were kind to someone? (After the child answers, say,"Hooray for you!")

Remember Rhyme

Keep it in mind to be sweet and kind.

27

Be Thoughtful

Let's Read the Picture

1. These two men are named Paul and Silas. Where are they?

2. Do you think Paul and Silas would be happy to get a letter from a friend?

3. When you write or call a friend, are you being thoughtful? Say, "Hooray for me!"

4. What other ways can you think of to be thoughtful to people?

5. Does it make Jesus happy when we are thoughtful and kind?

1. This little boy's name is Johnny. What is Johnny doing?

2. Who do you think Johnny is writing his letter to?

3. Is Johnny being kind and thoughtful? Say, "Hooray for Johnny!"

4. Does it make Johnny feel good to be thoughtful?

5. How can you tell that Johnny is feeling good?

6. Will it make you feel good to be kind and thoughtful too? Say, "Mmmmm, I feel *good*."

7. Does God want us to be thoughtful to others?

Remember Rhyme

It's delightful to be thoughtful.

29

Be Caring

Let's Read the Picture

1. This shepherd's name is David. How many baby lambs is David carrying?

2. What color are the little lambs?

3. These two little lambs have been lost. (Sing, "We are two little lambs, and we've lost our way. Baaa. Baaa. Baaa.")

4. What is David doing?

5. Do you think David cares about his little sheep? Say, "Hooray for David!"

6. Who else in the picture shows that she cares for a baby lamb? Say, "Hooray for Mama Sheep."

7. Is Jesus happy when we take care of other people?

8. Does Jesus take care of you? Say, "Thank you, Jesus."

"Care for one another." 1 Corinthians 12:25

1. What's wrong with the puppy in this picture? The puppy's name is Sugar.

2. Who is taking care of the puppy? Her name is Lauren. Say, "Hooray for Lauren!"

3. Is Sugar happy because Lauren is taking care of her foot?

4. Do *you* take care of your pets?

5. Tell about a time when you helped take care of one of your pets. (When the child is finished telling, say, "Hooray for you!")

6. Does God want us to take care of animals and people?

Remember Rhyme

It's always fair to show you care.

Be in Control

Let's Read the Picture

1. The woman in this picture is named Eve. The evil snake is named Satan. What is Satan doing?

2. Does the fruit look like it would taste good? Say, "Yum yum!"

3. Do you think Eve should take the fruit from Satan? Why not?

4. How could Eve control herself?

5. Is it good to have self-control?

6. When you see something you want, but you know you should not have it, what should you do?

7. What does God say when you have self-control? ("Hooray for you!")

"We should be awake and have self-control."
2 Thessalonians 5:6

1. This little girl is named Amanda. What color is Amanda's hair?

2. What is Amanda doing?

3. Can you point to Amanda's friends in this picture?

4. What are her friends doing?

5. Do you think Amanda would rather be playing her piano or playing with her friends?

6. Is Amanda showing self-control? Say, "Hooray for Amanda!"

7. Can you tell about a time when you had to have self-control? (After the child tells, say, "Hooray for you!")

Remember Rhyme

It's a wonderful goal to have self-control!

33

Be Good To Enemies

Let's Read the Picture

1. The man on the ground is a Jewish man. The other man is from the country of Samaria. Their countries are enemies.

2. What's wrong with the Jewish man on the ground? Say, "Awwww."

3. What is the Good Samaritan doing?

Say, "Hooray for the Good Samaritan!"

4. Is the Jewish man surprised by his enemy's kindness?

5. Is Jesus happy when we help our enemies?

6. Have you ever helped someone who is not your friend? (If the child says yes, say, "Hooray for you!")

"Love your enemies. Do good to them."
Luke 6:35

1. Tommy (the one standing) and Matthew are playing baseball, but they are on different teams. Say, "Go team!"

2. What color is Tommy's uniform? What color is Matthew's uniform?

3. Why is Matthew on the ground?

4. What is Tommy doing?

5. Is Tommy helping the boy on the other team? Say, "Hooray for Tommy!"

6. Why is Matthew smiling?

7. Is Jesus happy when you are nice to others?

Remember Rhyme   *Jumping Jimminies, don't be enemies!*

35

Don't Quit Doing Good

Let's Read the Picture

1. Why is this man jumping around and laughing? Say, "Hooray for Jesus!"

2. Is Jesus happy that he was able to help this crippled man?

3. Do you think Jesus was doing good when he helped this man?

4. Point to two men in the picture who are not happy.

5. Do you think they are angry with Jesus

6. Should Jesus stop doing good things because these men are upset with him?

7. Does Jesus want us always to do good, no matter what happens?

8. Tell about something good you have done. (When the child finishes, say, "Hooray for you!")

"I will never stop doing good."
Jeremiah 32:40

1. This girl is named Charlotte. Her friends call her Charlie. Her legs don't work just right, so she uses a wheel chair to play.

2. That woman is Charlie's mother. What is she doing?

3. What is Charlie doing to help her mother?

4. Is God proud of us when we help others?

5. Have you ever helped someone do a big job? (If the child says yes, say, "Hooray for you!")

Remember Rhyme

Good Christians should do lots of good.

Feed the Hungry

Let's Read the Picture

1. Jesus is in this picture. Can you point to him?

2. What are the people in this picture doing? Say, "Yum, yum."

3. Are most of the people happy?

4. Can you find some men who are *not* happy? They are Jesus' enemies.

5. Are the angry men eating, too?

6. Is Jesus feeding his hungry enemies? Say, "Hooray for Jesus!"

7. Does Jesus want *you* to feed hungry people and animals when you can?

"If your enemy is hungry, feed him." Romans 12:20

1. This little boy is named Austin, and his dad is named Joe. Where are they?

2. There are some poor, hungry people in this picture, too. Can you point to them? Say, "Awwww."

3. What are Austin and Joe doing? Say, "Hooray for Austin and Joe!"

4. Are the people happy to get the food? Say, "Ahh."

6. Will God be happy when you give food to hungry people?

7. Can you tell about a time when you gave food to someone who was hungry? (If the child says yes, say, "Hooray for you!")

Remember Rhyme

From Monday to Sunday, let's feed the hungry!

39

Be Giving

Let's Read the Picture

1. The woman in this picture is called a "widow." That means she no longer has a husband. Say, "Awwww."

2. What is the woman doing? Say, "Hooray for the widow!"

3. Is she giving *lots* of money?

4. Can you point to Jesus and his followers in the picture?

5. Why do you think Jesus is smiling at the woman?

6. Is Jesus happy because the woman is giving her money to God?

7. Will Jesus be happy if you give some of your money to God, too?

40

"It is more blessed to give than to receive."
Acts 20:35

1. Please point to the teacher in this picture. What color is the teacher's hair?

2. Can you count the children? How many are there?

3. Where are the children and teacher?

4. What are the children doing? Say, "Hooray for the children!"

5. The children are smiling. Does it make them happy to give their money to God?

6. Does it make you happy to give some of your money to God? (If the child says yes, say, "Hooray for you!")

7. The church can use the money you give to tell people about Jesus. Will that make God happy?

Remember Rhyme

Be happy to give; that's how to live!

Be Helpful

Let's Read the Picture

1. What is happening in this picture?

2. Why are the four friends carrying this man? Say, "Awwww."

3. Where are they taking him?

4. Are the men helping their sick friend? Say, "Hooray for the four friends!"

5. Who else in the picture is helping a weaker friend? Say, "Hooray for bunny!"

6. What color are the bunnies?

7. Can you wiggle your nose like a bunny does?

8. Have you ever helped a sick or hurt friend? (If the child says yes, say, "Hooray for you!")

"Help those who are weak."
1 Thessalonians 5:14

1. This boy's name is Harry. Say, "Hello, Harry."

2. The lady is named Grandmother Chang. Say, "Hello, Grandmother Chang."

3. What is Harry doing?

4. Is Harry helping her? Say, "Hooray for Harry!"

5. Do you ever help your mother carry the groceries?

(If the child says yes, say, "Hooray for you!")

6. Is Grandmother Chang happy that Harry is helping her?

7. Do you suppose Grandmother Chang has a surprise for Harry in one of her grocery bags? Say, "Oh boy!"

Remember Rhyme Never yelp when it's time to help!

43

Honor Others

Let's Read the Picture

1. Do you see a large animal in this picture?

2. What kind of animal is it? Say, "Hee haw!"

3. What color is the donkey?

4. Point to Jesus in the picture.

5. What are the people doing to *honor* Jesus? Say, "Hooray for the people!"

6. Who else in the crowd is *honoring* Jesus?

7. What sound does the kitten make?

8. What can *you* do to honor Jesus? (After the child tells, say, "Hooray for you!")

1. This is William and his sister, Betsy. Say, "Hello, William. Hello, Betsy."

2. William has pinned a ribbon on Betsy. What color is the ribbon Betsy is wearing?

3. The words on the ribbon say, "Number one sister." Is William honoring Betsy? Say, "Hooray for William!"

4. Why do you think Betsy is smiling?

5. Can you think of someone *you* would like to honor?

6. What could you do to honor that person?

7. Is Jesus happy when you honor your mom and dad?

Remember Rhyme

Honor fathers, honor mothers; it's so nice to honor others.

Be Humble

Let's Read the Picture

1. The man standing by the window is called a *Pharisee.* The man in the closet is called a *tax collector*.

2. What are both these men doing?

3. Point to the man you think is being humble. Say, "Hooray for the tax collector!"

4. What do you think it means to be humble?

5. Do you think the Pharisee is being humble? Say, "Boo for being proud."

6. Is God happy when we talk to him in prayer?

7. Let's talk to him right now.

"Always be humble and gentle."
Ephesians 4:2

1. These two girls are named Jenny and Carol. Say, "Hello, Jenny. Hello, Carol."

2. What have the girls been doing?

3. Jenny is showing off her eggs to Carol. How many eggs does Jenny have in her basket?

4. Do you think Jenny is being humble? Say, "Boo for being proud."

5. Carol is not showing off her eggs to Jenny. How many eggs does Carol have in her basket?

6. Do you think Carol is being humble? Say, "Hooray for Carol!"

7. Why do you think the teacher is smiling at Carol?

Remember Rhyme

Never brag; never grumble; just be sweet and, oh, so humble.

Be a Listener

Let's Read the Picture

1. Who do you think the man sitting in front of the other people is?

2. Say, "I love you, Jesus."

3. Jesus is holding a *scroll* in his hand. When Jesus lived the Bible was written on scrolls. Can you point to the scroll?

4. What is Jesus doing with the scroll?

5. How many people in the picture are listening to Jesus read? Let's count them.

6. Do you listen carefully when someone reads from the Bible? (If the child says yes, say, "Hooray for you!")

7. Are you listening to someone read right now? Say, "Hooray for me!"

"Always be willing to listen . . . ." James 1:19

Amys Summer

1. This little girl's name is Melinda. Say, "Hello, Melinda."

2. Melinda's grandmother is reading a bedtime story to her. Say, "Thank you, Grandmother."

3. What is Melinda doing? Say, "Hooray for Melinda!"

4. Who else in the picture is listening to Grandmother read?

5. Can you name the animals? What sounds do those animals make?

6. Is Grandmother happy because everyone is listening quietly?

7. What do you think God says when you listen carefully to his Book being read?

Remember Rhyme

Speaking once, but listening twice, makes your life so very nice!

Love God

Let's Read the Picture

1. These people are Christians. How many Christians can you count?

2. Do Christians love God?

3. What are these Christians doing? Say, "Hooray for the Christians!"

4. Why do you think these Christians are hiding to worship?

5. Do *you* love God, too? (If the child says yes, say, "Hooray for you!")

6. Do you think God smiles when you love him?

"Love the Lord your God with all your heart."
Matthew 22:37

1. Kera has fallen asleep. Say, "Sweet dreams, Kera."

2. Kera's friend, Snuggles, is next to her. What color is Snuggles?

3. What sound does Snuggles make?

4. What book does Kera have under her arms?

5. Can you point to the Bible? Say, "I love the Bible."

6. Whose words are in the Bible?

Remember Rhyme

It's
God I love
who's up above!

Make Peace

Let's Read the Picture

1. The beautiful woman in this picture is named Abigail. Say, "Hello, Abigail."

2. How many other people are in the picture? Can you count them?

3. The man who is smiling is named David. Abigail's husband was rude to David and made him angry. Say, "Boo on rude!"

4. What has Abigail brought to David and his men?

5. Is Abigail trying to make peace with David? Say, "Hooray for Abigail!"

6. When your friends become angry, do you try to make peace between them? (If the child says yes, say, "Hooray for you!")

"Those who work to bring peace are happy."
Matthew 5:9

1. Miguel and Tommy have been fighting over the clay. Say, "Boo on fighting!"

2. Does God like it when we fight?

3. What is their friend Jon doing? Say, "Hooray for Jon."

4. Are Miguel and Tommy glad to be making peace now?

5. Do you ever fight with your friends over toys?

6. How can you make peace with your friends?

Remember Rhyme

Never cease in making peace!

53

Obey

Let's Read the Picture

1. This man's name is Jonah. Say, "Hello, Jonah."

2. Jonah did not obey God. Say, "Oh no!"

3. So, where is Jonah now?

4. Does Jonah look happy? Say, "Awwww."

5. Is it always a good idea to obey God?

6. Do you see some other critters in the water with Jonah? What do you see?

7. Will you always try to obey God? (If the child says yes, say, "Hooray for you!")

1. Penny's mom asked Penny to clean up her room. Name some of the things that Penny did.

2. Penny's room is clean and neat, isn't it? Say, "Good job, Penny!"

3. Did Penny obey her mother? Say, "Hooray for Penny!"

4. Penny's mom gave her a special reward for obeying her. What was Penny's reward?

Say, "Mmmm mmm good."

5. Do you obey your mom when she asks you to do something? (If the child says yes, say, "Hooray for you!")

6. Is Jesus happy when you obey your parents and teachers?

Remember Rhyme

It's a happy day when I obey!

Be Patient

Let's Read the Picture

1. This man's name is Abraham. Can you say, "Abraham"?

2. Abraham's wife is named Sarah. Say, "Hello, Sarah."

3. God promised to send Abraham and Sarah a baby boy. So they waited . . . and waited . . . and waited. Do you think they were being patient? Say,

"Hooray for Abraham and Sarah!"

4. Finally, God sent them a little baby boy named Isaac. Let's sing a lullaby for the baby. (Sing "Lullaby and Goodnight" with your child.)

5. Did God bless Abraham and Sarah for being patient?

6. Are you patient when you have to wait for something special? (If the child says yes, say, "Hooray for you!")

"Be patient and accept each other with love."
Ephesians 4:2

1. Point to the ice cream truck in this picture.

2. Can you make a sound like the music of the ice cream truck?

3. Are these children waiting their turns patiently to buy ice cream? Say, "Hooray for the children!"

4. Who else in this picture wants some ice cream?

5. What color is the puppy?

6. When you go for ice cream, do you wait patiently? (If the child says yes, say, "Hooray for you!")

7. What is your favorite kind of ice cream?

Remember Rhyme

I will try to nicely wait, for patience is a happy trait.

Be Polite

Let's Read the Picture

1. The ten men in this picture have been very sick. Say, "Awwww."

2. Jesus made the ten men well. Say, "Thank you, Jesus."

3. One man has come back to thank Jesus for making him well. Is he being polite? Say, "Hooray for the polite man!"

4. Are the other nine men being polite? Say, "Boo for rudeness."

5. Do you say *please* and *thank you* when you should? (If the child says yes, say, "Hooray for you!")

6. When you want a cookie, what do you say to your mom?

7. When Mom gives you the cookie, what do you say?

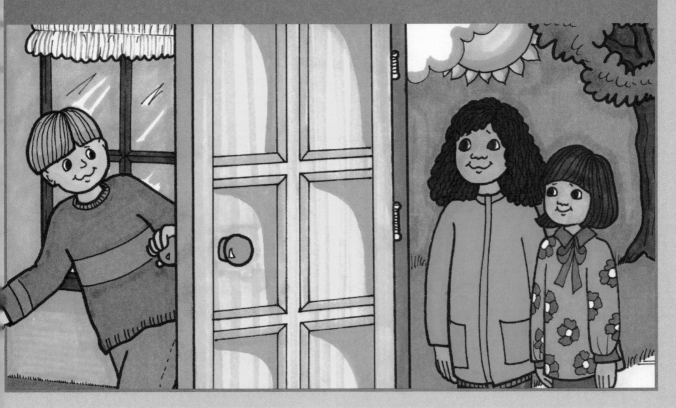

1. Tony is holding the door open for Jill and Sara. Say, "Hi Tony. Hi Jill and Sara."

2. Do you think Tony is being polite? Say, "Hooray for Tony!"

3. Are Jill and Sara smiling at Tony?

4. What do you think the girls will say to Tony?

5. Is Tony smiling, too? Does it make Tony feel good to be polite? Say, "Ahhhh, that feels nice."

6. Who is happy when *you* are polite?

Remember Rhyme

It's always right to be polite.

Be Full of Praise

Let's Read the Picture

1. Point to the shepherd in this picture. His name is David.

2. What is David doing?

3. Who do you think David is singing about?

4. Can you sing a song about God, too? (Sing, "God Is So Good" or some other praise song the child likes.)

5. Does God like to hear you sing about him? Say, "Hooray for me!"

6. Who else in the picture likes to hear David sing?

7. Do you like for someone to sing to you when it's time to go to sleep?

1. Bobby is painting a pretty picture, isn't he?

2. What is in Bobby's picture?

3. Do you think Bobby's painting praises God? Say, "Hooray for Bobby!"

4. What do *you* like to do to praise God? (If the child answers appropriately, say, "Hooray for you!")

5. When you go to Sunday school, does your class praise God?

6. Would you like to draw a picture to praise God right now? (Let the child color or draw a picture of a landscape.)

Remember Rhyme

Happy days are full of praise!

Always Pray

Let's Read the Picture

1. Where is Jesus in this picture?

2. Is it daytime or nighttime?

3. What is Jesus doing? Say, "Hooray for Jesus!"

4. What does it mean to pray to God?

5. Are Jesus' friends praying, too? Say, "Oh no!"

6. What are they doing? Pretend that you are snoring and say, "Zzzzzz zzzzzz."

7. Does Jesus want you to pray, too? Let's pray right now. (Pray with the child.)

"Pray without stopping." I Thessalonians 5:17

1. This is the Juarez family. Say, "Hello, Juarez family."

2. How many people are in this family? Can you count them?

3. What are they doing? Say, "Hooray for the Juarez family!"

4. Who else in the picture seems to be praying?

5. What sounds do cats and kittens make?

6. Why do you pray before you eat?

7. Do you always pray before you eat? (If the child says yes, say, "Hooray for you!")

Remember Rhyme

I love to pray; it makes my day!

63

Protect the Earth

Let's Read the Picture

1. This man's name is Adam. And the woman's name is Eve. Say, "Hello Adam and Eve."

2. Adam and Eve are in the Garden of Eden. What colors do you see in the garden?

3. What is Adam doing?

4. What is Eve doing?

5. Are Adam and Eve protecting the earth by taking care of it? Say, "Hooray for Adam and Eve!"

6. Who else is taking care of the garden?

7. What are they taking care of? Can you say, "Chomp, chomp"?

"God put the man in the garden to tend it."
Genesis 2:15

1. Peter and his dad are planting a tree in their yard. What color are the leaves of the tree?

2. Are Peter and his dad helping to protect the earth? Say, "Hooray for Peter and his dad!"

3. Who else in the picture is planting something?

4. How many squirrels are there?

5. What are the squirrels planting?

6. When an acorn grows up, what does it become?

7. Is God happy when you help take care of the earth?

Remember Rhyme

Take care of Earth; it has great worth!

Remember the Lord

Let's Read the Picture

1. This man's name is Moses. He was once the leader of God's people. Say, "Hello Moses."

2. Moses is remembering how God helped his people. Is it good to remember God? Say, "Hooray for Moses!"

3. Point to the dry path in the middle of the water in this picture.

4. God made the dry path through the water. Isn't God wonderful?

5. Can you remember something good about God? (When the child answers appropriately, say, "Hooray for you!")

6. Let's pray and tell God right now that we remember him. (Pray with the child.)

1. This is the Williams family. How many people are in this family?

2. They are sharing a holiday meal. Can you guess which holiday it is? Say, "Yum yum!"

3. Can you name some of the foods on the table?

4. What are the Williams doing right now?

5. What do you think they are saying to God?

6. Are the Williams remembering how good God has been to them? Say, "Hooray for the Williams family!"

7. Are you thankful to God for the good things he does for you? (If the child says yes, say, "Hooray for you!")

Remember Rhyme

From January to December, it's God we remember!

Be Respectful

Let's Read the Picture

1. Can you point to the mountain in this picture?

2. God is on the mountain. Say, "God is so wonderful!"

3. What are God's people in this picture doing?

4. Do you think they are bowing down because they respect God? Say, "Hooray for God's people!"

5. What does it mean to *respect* someone?

6. Do *you* respect God? (If the child says yes, say, "Hooray for you!")

7. Who else do you respect?

"Show respect for all people...
respect God." I Peter 2:17

1. Chad and Robby are baseball players. Say, "Hello Chad and Robby."

2. Coach Bill is letting Chad and Robby meet some of his friends. Why are Chad and Robby holding their hats in their hands? Say, "Hooray for Chad and Robby!"

3. Are the man and woman happy that Chad and Robby are showing respect to them?

4. Is the coach happy, too?

5. How can you show respect to older people?

Remember Rhyme

People expect to be shown respect!

Say No

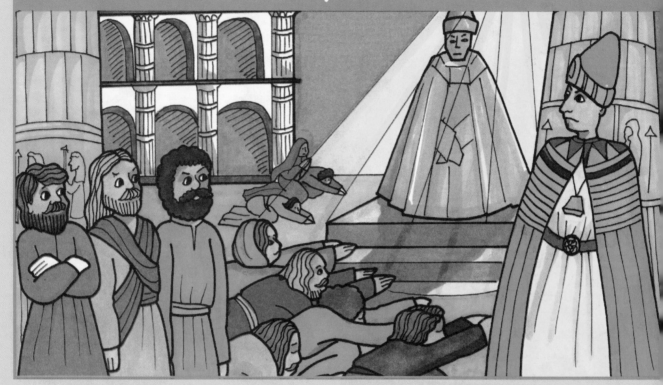

Let's Read the Picture

1. Point to the king in this picture. Does he look happy?

2. There is a false god in this picture. What color is the big false god?

3. The king told all the people to bow down and worship this false god. Is it right to worship a *false* god? Say, "Boo on false gods!"

4. These three men said no to the king. Their names are Shadrach, Meshach, and Abednego. Are they bowing down to the false god? Say, "Hooray for God's men!"

5. Who are *you* supposed to worship?

6. Should you always say no when someone asks you to do something wrong?

"Respect the Lord and refuse to do wrong."
Proverbs 3:7

1. Chen is trying to start a fight with Larry. Say, "Boo for fighting!"

2. Do you think Larry said no to fighting Chen? Say, "Hooray for Larry!"

3. Does anyone ever try to start a fight with you? (If the child says yes, say, "Boo on fighting!")

4. What should you *say* if someone wants to fight?

5. What should you *do* if someone wants to fight?

6. Does Jesus like for people to fight with one another?

Remember Rhyme

Just say no when it's wrong, you know?

71

Be a Servant

Let's Read the Picture

1. How many men are in this picture? They are called apostles. Can you count them?

2. Point to Jesus in the picture.

3. What is Jesus doing?

4. Do you think Jesus is serving the apostle? Say, "Hooray for Jesus!"

5. What can *you* do to serve someone else? (When the child answers appropriately, say, "Hooray for you!")

6. Does it make God happy when you serve someone else?

7. Do you feel good when you serve someone? Say, "Ahh, I feel so good."

"Through love serve one another." Galatians 5:13

1. Can you tell what's happening in this picture?

2. Are the people serving the food doing what Jesus wants us to do? Say, "Hooray for the servants!"

3. Who else in the picture is serving someone?

4. Are the people *serving* the food happy? How can you tell?

5. Are the people *being served* happy, too?

6. Can you think of a time when you served someone else? (When the child tells, say, "Hooray for you!")

Remember Rhyme *Sisters and brothers should serve one another.*

Share

Let's Read the Picture

1. Point to the baby in the picture. What is the baby's name?

2. Some wise men are in the picture. Can you count them?

3. What are the wise men doing? Say, "Hooray for the wise men!"

4. Is Jesus happy?

5. Who else in the picture is sharing?

6. Do you have something you can share with Jesus? (If the child answers appropriately, say, "Hooray for you!")

7. Let's share a song right now. (Sing, "It Isn't Any Trouble Just to S-H-A-R-E.")

"Do not forget to . . . share with them."
Hebrews 13:16

1. Point to the girl with light hair in the picture. Her name is Bonnie. What has she been doing?

2. Point to the girl with dark hair. Her name is Joy. What is wrong with Joy? Say, "Awwww."

3. Is Bonnie being nice to Joy? How do you know? Say, "Hooray for Bonnie!"

4. Does Joy look happy? Why do you think she is happy?

5. Does Bonnie look happy, too? Why do you think she is happy?

6. Who else in the picture is sharing?

7. If you had something special, would you share it with a friend? (If the child says yes, say, "Hooray for you!")

Remember Rhyme

When I share I show I care.

75

Stay Away from Evil

Let's Read the Picture

1. Stephen is a good man, but people are being mean to him in this picture. Can you point to Stephen?

2. Saul is watching the men be mean to Stephen. Where is Saul in the picture?

3. Is Saul doing the right thing by watching these men be mean? Say, "Boo for being mean!"

4. Can you find the young man who is running away from evil? Say, "Hooray for running away from evil!"

5. When *you* see something evil, what should you do?

6. If someone asks you to help them do evil, what should you say?

"Stand against the devil." James 4:7

1. There is an evil gang of boys in this picture. Can you count them?

2. What colors do you see in this picture?

3. Danny has decided to join the gang. Say, "Boo for bad gangs!"

4. Ricardo has decided not to join the evil gang. Say, "Hooray for Ricardo!"

5. What should you do if someone wants you to be in a gang?

6. Do you think Jesus would be in a gang? Say, "Hooray for Jesus!"

Remember Rhyme *When evil comes to play, I always run away!*

Study God's Word

Let's Read the Picture

1. This man makes copies of God's Word. He is called a scribe. Say, "Hello, Mr. Scribe."

2. He uses several tools as he works. Can you name some of his tools in the picture?

3. Do you think this man studies God's Word carefully every day? Say, "Hooray for the scribe!"

4. Is it a good thing to study God's Word?

5. Do you have a copy of the Bible, God's Word, of your very own? (If the child says yes, say, "Hooray for you!")

6. Let's get your Bible and read some-thing from it right now. (Read John 3:16 from the child's Bible.)

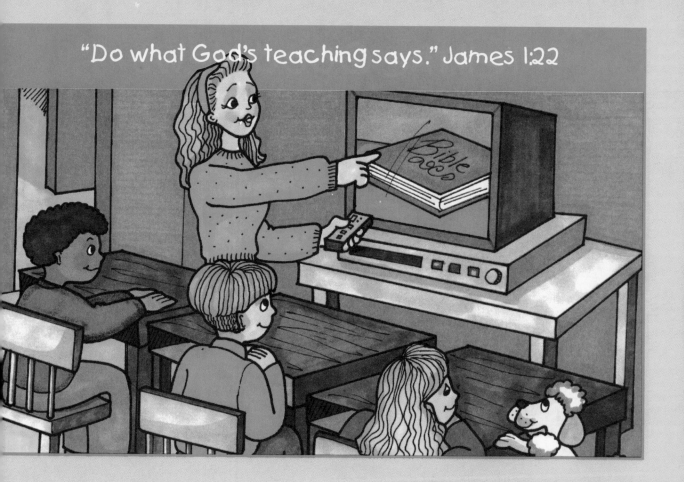

"Do what God's teaching says." James 1:22

1. These children are in Sunday school class. Can you point to the teacher?

2. How many children are in the picture? Let's count them.

3. What are the children doing?

4. What is the video about?

5. Are the children studying God's Word? Say, "Hooray for the children!"

6. Is God happy when *you* study his Word?

Remember Rhyme

Don't be a nerd; study God's Word!

79

Tell the Good News

Let's Read the Picture

1. There is some Good News in the Bible. The Good News is that Jesus came to save us. Say, "Thank you, Jesus."

2. Can you point to Jesus in this picture?

3. What colors do you see in the picture?

4. Do you think Jesus is telling these people about the Good News? Say, "Hooray for Jesus!"

5. How do you know he is telling them Good News? ·

6. Do you like to get good news, too?

7. Tell about a time when you got some good news.

8. Let's sing, "Jesus Loves Me."

"I want ... to preach the Good News ..."
Romans 1:15

1. This little boy is named Monty. Say, "Hello, Monty."

2. Monty wants to be a preacher someday so he can tell people the Good News about Jesus. Say, "Hooray for Monty!"

3. How many birds are listening to Monty preach?

4. What colors are the birds?

5. Who else is listening to the Good News about Jesus?

6. Have you told your best friend about Jesus? (If the child says yes, say, "Hooray for you!")

Remember Rhyme

I always choose to tell the Good News!

81

Be Truthful

Let's Read the Picture

1. Jesus did not do anything wrong, but he is on trial. Say, "Awwww."

2. Can you point to the judge?

3. Do you think the man pointing at Jesus is telling the truth about him? Say, "Boo on lying!"

4. Is it ever right to tell a lie?

5. Does Jesus want you to always tell the truth? Say, "Hooray for truth!"

6. When *you* do something wrong, do you tell the truth anyway? (If the child says yes, say, "Hooray for you!")

"You must stop telling lies. Tell each other the truth ..."
Ephesians 4:25

1. Donna is sad in this picture. Is Donna in trouble with her mom? Say, "Awwww."

2. What did Donna do wrong?

3. But is Donna telling her mom the truth? Say, "Hooray for Donna!"

4. Who else has been dressing up in this picture? Say, "Meow."

5. What color is the hat on the cat?

6. Do you ever dress up in your mom's or dad's clothes?

7. When you get caught doing something wrong, what should you do?

Remember Rhyme

Telling lies will make you sad, but telling truth will make you glad.

Be Thankful

Let's Read the Picture

1. There's a rainbow in this picture. Can you point to it?

2. What colors do you see in the rainbow?

3. Where is Noah in the picture?

4. Can you find Noah's big boat in the picture?

5. What animals do you see? What sounds do the animals make?

6. What are Noah and his family doing?

7. Do you think they are thankful that God has saved them? Say, "Thank you, God."

"Always give thanks to God the Father for everything."
Ephesians 5:20

1. Sonny's family is having a picnic in the park. Where is the checkered tablecloth?

2. What is Sonny's family doing right now?

3. Do you think they are thanking God for the nice foods? Say, "Hooray for Sonny's family!"

4. Who else in the picture is eating good food?

5. What color are the ducks?

6. Does your family pray and thank God for your food before meals? (If the child says yes, say, "Hooray for you!")

When I bow my head and pray, I give thanks to God each day.

Remember Rhyme

85

Be Trusting

Let's Read the Picture

1. How many lions can you count in this picture?

2. Do the lions look hungry? Say, "Roar!"

3. The guards are going to put Daniel in the pit with the lions. Say, "Oh no!"

4. But does Daniel look afraid?

5. Will God protect Daniel from the lions? Say, "Thank you, God."

6. Do you think Daniel trusts God to save him? Say, "Hooray for Daniel!"

7. Let's sing, "Daniel In the Lion's Den."

"Lord my God, I trust in you . . ." Psalm 7:1

1. Mr. Wong is helping his son Ty learn to swim. Say, "Splash, splash!"

2. Is Ty having fun? How can you tell?

3. Why isn't Ty afraid?

4. Does Ty trust his dad to keep him safe? Say, "Hooray for Ty!"

5. Who else in this picture is learning something new?

6. What color is the baby bird?

7. Does the baby bird trust its mother? Say, "Hooray for the baby bird!"

8. Do you trust God to take care of you, too? (If the child says yes, say, "Hooray for you!")

Remember Rhyme

It's a must in God to trust!

Be a Worker

Let's Read the Picture

1. The woman in this picture is named Ruth. The man watching her is named Boaz. Say, "Hello Ruth and Boaz."

2. Is Ruth working very hard in the hot sun? Say, "Hooray for Ruth!"

3. What is Ruth doing?

4. Is Boaz happy with the work Ruth is doing? How can you tell?

5. Do you have work to do, too? What kind of work do you have to do?

6. Is your mom or dad happy when you do your work? Say, "Hooray for you!"

7. God gave us work to do. Say, "Thank you, God, for work."

1. These children are named Rita and Roberto. Which one is Rita? Which one is Roberto?

2. What are the children doing?

3. Do families have to work together to have a happy home?

4. Who else in this picture is working?

5. What does the parrot say?

6. Do you like to work and help your mom or dad? (If the child says yes, say, "Hooray for you!")

7. Let's sing "Whistle While You Work."

Remember Rhyme

A little work, a little play, makes life happy day by day!

Worship

Let's Read the Picture

1. This is a picture of heaven. Can you point to the angels?

2. Which angels are flying? Which angels are bowing down?

3. Are the angels worshipping God? Say, "Hooray for the angels!"

4. Is God happy when you worship him, too?

5. When do you worship God? (When the child answers appropriately, say, "Hooray for you!")

6. God is like a wonderful light. Can you point to the light in the picture?

7. Who else is worshipping God?

"You must worship the Lord your God." Matthew 4:10

1. How many children do you see around this campfire?

2. What colors can you see in the fire?

3. What are the children doing?

4. Are they worshipping God? Say, "Hooray for the children!"

5. Do you think the children are happy?

6. Are you happy when you worship God? (If the child says yes, say, "Hooray for you!")

7. (Help the child to worship God by singing a song and praying.)

Remember Rhyme *Get on board and worship the Lord!*

Index of Bible Stories

Bible Story	Page